D0846671

THE BOOK
OF
HOURS

POEMS FROM THE BOOK of HOURS

"Das STUNDENBUCH"

By RAINER MARIA RILKE TRANSLATED BY BABETTE DEUTSCH

A New Directions Book

Copyright 1941 by New Directions Publishing Corporation
Library of Congress Catalog Card Number: 42–21208

All rights reserved. Except for brief passages quoted in a newspaper, magazine, radio, or television review, no part of this book may be reproduced in any form or by any means, electronic or mechanical, including photocopying and recording, or by any information storage and retrieval system, without permission in writing from the Publisher.

Manufactured in the United States of America
Originally published by New Directions in 1941 in the Poets of the Year Series; designed by Peter Beilenson
First published as New Directions Paperbook 408 (ISBN: 0-8112-0595-9) in 1975
Published simultaneously in Canada by George J. McLeod Ltd., Toronto

New Directions Books are published for James Laughlin
by New Directions Publishing Corporation,
80 Eighth Avenue, New York 10011.

FIFTH PRINTING

CONTENTS

PREFACE

Rﾃ桁KE's Bﾃ闔K ﾃ僘 Hﾃ伯RS falls into three parts: The Book of Monkish Life, composed in the autumn of 1899; The Book of Pilgrimage, composed two years later, and The Book of Poverty and Death, the work of an April week in 1903. The first two parts were also written in a burst of creative energy, the one in a little less than a month, the other in ten days. In spite of the ease with which these lyrics flowed from his pen, however, Rilke felt when he had completed them that he had still to find himself as a poet. Yet this comparatively early volume contains the germ of his mature convictions and, in the richness of its harmonies and the suggestiveness of its imagery, bears his unique signature.

It was in Italy that he composed both the first and the final section of the book, and in Germany that he wrote the second, but though there are references to Italian places and persons in certain poems, and to the landscape of Westerwede in others, the genius loci that presides over the book is primarily that of Russia and that of Paris. The poet felt Russia, which he had visited just prior to the writing of the first section, to be his spiritual home, and so the monk who is the imaginary author of the poems is represented as an adherent of the peculiar faith that Rilke ascribed to his spiritual kinsmen, a faith in a God remote from the august if benign Father of western Christianity, a God, rather, who was waiting to be born of the artist's alert and sensitive consciousness. Again, in the last section of the book, the poet is preoccupied by the horror with which the more squalid aspects of Paris assaulted him, and devotes himself to celebrating the Franciscan ideal of poverty and the divinity with which he invested death. The meanness of existence in the great cities, above all, the insignificance of death for the anonymous masses there, was his chief theme. Thus the third part of THE BOOK OF HOURS is something in the nature of an apostrophe to the God who will grant men their individual and personal deaths. Although this idea has particular cogency at a time like the present,* no lyrics from this section are offered here, as unfortunately they do not readily lend themselves to translation. Certain of the poems in the dozen chosen from The Book of Monkish Life and in the group selected from The Book of Pilgrimage do convey, however, if somewhat obliquely, the spirit that informs the later lyrics.

The poems allow of interpretations acceptable both to the pious and the philosophical mind. Aside from one lyric alive with the erotic quality pervading a large part of such verse, the work distinguishes itself from the religious poetry with which we are familiar. Rilke, as is well known, was hostile to orthodox Christianity, to the churches that "encircle God as though / he were a fugitive, and then bewail him / as if he were a captured wounded creature." Yet there are hints here that he might have assented, with only slight reservations, to some of the ideas of that most devout of religious poets, the Jesuit priest, Gerard Manley Hopkins. One recalls a passage in a letter that Hopkins wrote to Bridges when trying, vainly as it proved, to convince him of the validity of the Catholic position. "To you it comes to: Christ is in some sense God, in some sense he is not God—

* Written in 1940, the phrase remains valid in 1968.

and your interest is in the uncertainty; to the Catholic it is: Christ is in every sense God and in every sense man, and the interest is in the locked and inseparable combination, or rather it is in the person in whom the combination has its place. Therefore we speak of the events of Christ's life as the mystery of the Nativity, the mystery of the Crucifixion and so on of a host; the mystery being always the same, that the child in the manger is God, the culprit on the gallows is God, and so on." Rilke might perhaps have reversed this, saying: "God is the child in the manger, the culprit on the gallows," since for him Deity, never clearly defined but profoundly felt, was all that demands our cherishing, our shamed pity, our dedication. Again, in an address based on the Spiritual Exercises of the founder of his Order, Hopkins wrote: "It is not only prayer that gives God glory but work. Smiting on an anvil, sawing a beam, whitewashing a wall, driving horses, sweeping, scouring, everything gives God some glory if being in his grace you do it as your duty. To go to communion worthily gives God great glory, but to take food in thankfulness and temperance gives him glory too. To lift up the hands in prayer gives God glory, but a man with a dungfork in his hand, a woman with a sloppail, give him glory too. He is so great that all things give him glory if you mean they should. So then, my brethren, live."

Rilke would not have been apt to exalt duty, with its cramping absoluteness, and he would have had small concern with going to communion in the prescribed fashion, but he might well have acknowledged the godliness of the man with the dungfork and the woman with the sloppail. And what else is the meaning of such a poem as that which begins: "All will grow great and powerful again" but Hopkins's admonition: "So then, my brethren, live"?

Certainly the Deity invoked in these poems is no distant and supernal power, but one close to the adorable humanity adumbrated in Blake's Everlasting Gospel. The God whom THE BOOK OF HOURS celebrates is not the Creator of the universe, but seems rather the creation of mankind, and above all, of that most intensely conscious part of mankind, the artists. He is present and to be revered in all that "truly lives," but he is not yet perfected; in a sense, he is also the future, the incomplete, the unachieved, the cathedral still in the building, the wine that has not yet ripened. Only by a more sensitive approach to life, and to things, which have a strange secret life of their own, as every artist feels, only by an effort to understand the death that every life carries within it like a seed, shall men, tutored by the artists among them, slowly realize this great unorthodox godhead.

The poems, presented here in the order in which they occur in the German text, were chosen first for their own sake and then because they seemed more amenable than others to transplanting in foreign soil. While the sense has not been sacrificed to the exigencies of the pattern, the translator's effort was to carry over into the English verse as much as the language allowed of the original music. The text of this second edition has undergone revision and includes several poems not published in the earlier selection.

B. D.

NOTE

The present edition contains a few revisions of the English versions included in the first edition, as well as five new translations. The order of the poems follows that in the original.

THE BOOK
OF
HOURS

a neigt sich die Stunde
und rührt mich an
mit klarem, metallenem Schlag:
mir zittern die Sinne. Ich fühle: ich kann—
und ich fasse den plastischen Tag.

Nichts war noch vollendet, eh ich es erschaut,
ein jedes Werden stand still.
Meine Blicke sind reif, und wie eine Braut
kommt jedem das Ding, das er will.

Nichts ist mir zu klein, und ich lieb es trotzdem
und mal' es auf Goldgrund und gross
und halte es hoch, und ich weiss nicht wem
löst es die Seele los . . .

Now the hour bows down, it touches me, throbs
metallic, lucid and bold:
my senses are trembling. I feel my own power—
on the plastic day I lay hold.

Until I perceived it, no thing was complete,
but waited, hushed, unfulfilled.
My vision is ripe, to each glance like a bride
comes softly the thing that was willed.

There is nothing too small, but my tenderness paints
it large on a background of gold,
and I prize it, not knowing whose soul at the sight,
released, may unfold . . .

Du, Nachbar Gott, wenn ich dich manches mal
in langer Nacht mit hartem Klopfen störe,—
so ists, weil ich dich selten atmen höre
und weiss: Du bist allein im Saal.
Und wenn du etwas brauchst, ist keiner da,
um deinem Tasten einen Trank zu reichen:
ich horche immer. Gib ein kleines Zeichen.
Ich bin ganz nah.

Nur eine schmale Wand ist zwischen uns,
durch Zufall; denn es könnte sein:
ein Rufen deines oder meines Munds—
und sie bricht ein
ganz ohne Lärm und Laut.

Aus deinen Bildern ist sie aufgebaut.

Und deine Bilder stehn vor dir wie Namen.
Und wenn einmal das Licht in mir entbrennt,
mit welchem meine Tiefe dich erkennt,
vergeudet sichs als Glanz auf ihren Rahmen.

Und meine Sinne, welche schnell erlahmen,
sind ohne Heimat und von dir getrennt.

You, neighbor God, if sometimes in the night
I rouse you with loud knocking, I do so
only because I seldom hear you breathe
and know: you are alone.
And should you need a drink, no one is there
to reach it to you, groping in the dark.
Always I hearken. Give but a small sign.
I am quite near.

Between us there is but a narrow wall,
and by sheer chance; for it would take
merely a call from your lips or from mine
to break it down,
and that without a sound.

The wall is builded of your images.

They stand before you hiding you like names,
And when the light within me blazes high
that in my inmost soul I know you by,
the radiance is squandered on their frames.

And then my senses, which too soon grow lame,
exiled from you, must go their homeless ways.

Wenn es nur einmal so ganz stille wäre.
Wenn das Zufällige und Ungefähre
verstummte und das nachbarliche Lachen,
wenn das Geräusch, das meine Sinne machen,
mich nicht so sehr verhinderte am Wachen—

Dann könnte ich in einem tausendfachen
Gedanken bis an deinen Rand dich denken
und dich besitzen (nur ein Lächeln lang),
um dich an alles Leben zu verschenken
wie einen Dank.

If only there were stillness, full, complete.
If all the random and approximate
were muted, with neighbors' laughter, for your sake,
and if the clamor that my senses make
did not confound the vigil I would keep—

Then in a thousandfold thought I could think
you out, even to your utmost brink,
and (while a smile endures) possess you, giving
you away, as though I were but giving thanks,
to all the living.

𝕴ch lese es heraus aus deinem 𝖂ort,
aus der Geschichte der Gebärden,
mit welchen deine Hände um das Werden
sich ründeten, begrenzend, warm und weise.
Du sagtest leben laut und sterben leise
und wiederholtest immer wieder: Sein.
Doch vor dem ersten Tode kam der Mord.
Da ging ein Riss durch deine reifen Kreise
und ging ein Schrein
und riss die Stimmen fort,
die eben erst sich sammelten,
um dich zu sagen,
um dich zu tragen,
alles Abgrunds Brücke—

Und was sie seither stammelten,
sind Stücke
deines alten Names.

𝕴 read it in your word, and learn it from
the history of the gestures of your warm
wise hands, rounding themselves to form
and circumscribe the shapes that are to come.
Aloud you said: to live, and low: to die,
and you repeated, tirelessly: to be.
And yet there was no death till murder came.
Then through your perfect circles ran a rent
and a cry tore,
scattering the voices that not long before
had gently blent
to utter you,
to carry you,
bridge across the abyss—

And what they since have stammered
are the fragments only
of your old name.

Ich bin, du Ängstlicher. Hörst du mich nicht
mit allen meinen Sinnen an dir branden?
Meine Gefühle, welche Flügel fanden,
umkreisen weiss dein Angesicht.
Siehst du nicht meine Seele, wie sie dicht
vor dir in einem Kleid aus Stille steht?
Reift nicht mein mailiches Gebet
an deinem Blicke wie an einem Baum?

Wenn du der Träumer bist, bin ich dein Traum.
Doch wenn du wachen willst, bin ich dein Wille
und werde mächtig aller Herrlichkeit
und ründe mich wie eine Sternenstille
über der wunderlichen Stadt der Zeit.

𝕴 am, you anxious one. Do you not hear me
rush to claim you with each eager sense?
Now my feelings have found wings, and, circling,
whitely fly about your countenance.
Here my spirit in its dress of stillness
stands before you,—oh, do you not see?
In your glance does not my Maytime prayer
grow to ripeness as upon a tree?

Dreamer, it is I who am your dream.
But would you awake, I am your will,
and master of all splendor, and I grow
to a sphere, like stars poised high and still,
with time's singular city stretched below.

Mein Leben ist nicht diese steile Stunde,
darin du mich so eilen siehst.
Ich bin ein Baum vor meinem Hintergrunde,
ich bin nur einer meiner vielen Munde
und jener, welcher sich am frühsten schliesst.

Ich bin die Ruhe zwischen zweien Tönen,
die sich nur schlecht aneinander gewöhnen:
denn der Ton Tod will sich erhöhn—

Aber im dunklen Intervall versöhnen
sich beide zitternd.
                    Und das Lied bleibt schön.

No, my life is not this precipitous hour
through which you see me passing at a run.
I stand before my background like a tree.
Of all my many mouths I am but one,
and that which soonest chooses to be dumb.

I am the rest between two notes
which, struck together, sound discordantly,
because death's note would claim a higher key.

But in the dark pause, trembling, the notes meet,
harmonious.
               And the song continues sweet.

Wenn ich gewachsen wäre irgendwo,
wo leichtere Tage sind und schlanke Stunden,
ich hätte dir ein grosses Fest erfunden,
und meine Hände hielten dich nicht so,
wie sie dich manchmal halten, bang und hart.

Dort hätte ich gewagt, dich zu vergeuden,
du grenzenlose Gegenwart.
Wie einen Ball
hätt ich dich in alle wogenden Freuden
hineingeschleudert, dass einer dich finge
und deinem Fall
mit hohen Händen entgegen springe,
du Ding der Dinge.

Ich hätte dich wie eine Klinge
blitzen lassen.
Vom goldensten Ringe
liess ich dein Feuer umfassen,
und er müsste mirs halten
über die weisseste Hand.

Gemalt hätt ich dich: nicht an die Wand,
an den Himmel selber von Rand zu Rand,
und hätt dich gebildet, wie ein Gigant

22

𝔍𝔣 𝔍 had grown up in a land where days
were free from care and hours were delicate,
then I would have contrived a splendid fête
for you, and not have held you in the way
I sometimes do, tightly in fearful hands.

There I would have been bold to squander you,
you boundless Presence.
Like a ball
I would have flung you among all tossing joys,
so one might catch you,
and if you seemed to fall,
with both hands high would spring
toward you,
you thing of things.

I would have let you flash
forth like a sword.
From the most golden of all rings
I would have taken your fire and
reset it in a mounting that would hold it
over the whitest hand.

I would have painted you: not on the wall,
but upon very heaven from verge to verge,
and would have shaped you, as a giant would:

23

dich bilden würde: als Berg, als Brand,
als Samum, wachsend aus Wüstensand—
oder
es kann auch sein: ich fand
dich einmal ...
                    Meine Freunde sind weit,
ich höre kaum noch ihr Lachen schallen;
und du: du bist aus dem Nest gefallen,
bist ein junger Vogel mit gelben Krallen
und grossen Augen und tust mir leid.
(Meine Hand ist dir viel zu breit).
Und ich heb mit dem Finger vom Quell einen Tropfen
und lausche, ob du ihn lechzend langst,
und ich fühle dein Herz und meines klopfen
und beide aus Angst.

you, as a mountain, as a blazing fire,
as the simoon, grown from the desert's surge—
or
it may be, in very truth, I found
you once . . .
My friends are far away,
I scarcely hear their laughter any more;
and you: ah, you have fallen from the nest,
a fledgling, yellow-clawed and with big eyes:
I grieve for you.
(In my broad hand your tininess is lost).
And from the well I lift a drop
upon my finger, intent if you'll stretch
a thirsty throat for it, and then I hear
your heart and mine beating,
and both with fear.

Ich finde dich in allen diesen Dingen,
denen ich gut und wie ein Bruder bin;
als Samen sonnst du dich in den geringen,
und in den grossen gibst du gross dich hin.

Das ist das wundersame Spiel der Kräfte,
dass sie so dienend durch die Dinge gehn:
in Wurzeln wachsend, schwindend in die Schäfte
und in den Wipfeln wie ein Auferstehn.

In all these things I cherish as a brother
still it is you I find; seedlike you wait,
basking serenely in the narrowest compass,
and greatly give yourself in what is great.

This is the marvel of the play of forces,
that they so serve the things wherethrough they flow:
growing in roots, to dwindle in the tree-trunks,
and in the crowns like resurrection show.

Werkleute sind wir: Knappen, Jünger, Meister,
und bauen dich, du hohes Mittelschiff.
Und manchmal kommt ein ernster Hergereister,
geht wie ein Glanz durch unsre hundert Geister
und zeigt uns zitternd einen neuen Griff.

Wir steigen in die wiegenden Gerüste,
in unsern Händen hängt der Hammer schwer,
bis eine Stunde uns die Stirnen küsste,
die strahlend und als ob sie alles wüsste
von dir kommt wie der Wind vom Meer.

Dann ist ein Hallen von dem vielen Hämmern,
und durch die Berge geht es Stoss um Stoss.
Erst wenn es dunkelt, lassen wir dich los:
Und deine kommenden Konturen dämmern.

Gott, du bist gross.

We are all workmen: prentice, journeyman,
or master, building you—you towering nave.
And sometimes there will come to us a grave
wayfarer, who like a radiance thrills
the souls of all our hundred artisans,
trembling as he shows us a new skill.

We climb up on the rocking scaffolding,
the hammers in our hands swing heavily,
until our foreheads feel the caressing wing
of a radiant hour that knows everything,
and hails from you as wind hails from the sea.

Then hammerstrokes sound, multitudinous,
and through the mountains echoes blast on blast.
Only at dusk we yield you up at last:
and slow your shaping contours dawn on us.

God, you are vast.

Was wirst du tun, Gott, wenn ich sterbe?
Ich bin dein Krug (wenn ich zerscherbe?)
Ich bin dein Trank (wenn ich verderbe?)
Bin dein Gewand und dein Gewerbe,
mit mir verlierst du deinen Sinn.

Nach mir hast du kein Haus, darin
dich Worte, nah und warm, begrüssen.
Es fällt von deinen müden Füssen
die Samtsandale, die ich bin.

Dein grosser Mantel lässt dich los.
Dein Blick, den ich mit meiner Wange
warm, wie mit einem Pfühl, empfange,
wird kommen, wird mich suchen, lange—
und legt beim Sonnenuntergange
sich fremden Steinen in den Schoss.

Was wirst du tun, Gott? Ich bin bange.

What will you do, God, when I die?
When I, your pitcher, broken, lie?
When I, your drink, go stale or dry?
I am your garb, the trade you ply,
you lose your meaning, losing me.

Homeless without me, you will be
robbed of your welcome, warm and sweet.
I am your sandals: your tired feet
will wander bare for want of me.

Your mighty cloak will fall away.
Your glance that on my cheek was laid
and pillowed warm, will seek, dismayed,
the comfort that I offered once—
to lie, as sunset colors fade
in the cold lap of alien stones.

What will you do, God? I am afraid.

Dein allererstes Wort war: Licht:
da ward die Zeit. Dann schwiegst du lange.
Dein zweites Wort ward Mensch und bange
(wir dunkeln noch in seinem Klange),
und wieder sinnt dein Angesicht.

Ich aber will dein drittes nicht.

Ich bete nachts oft: Sei der Stumme,
der wachsend in Gebärden bleibt
und den der Geist im Traume treibt,
dass er des Schweigens schwere Summe
in Stirnen und Gebirge schreibt.

Sei du die Zuflucht vor dem Zorne,
der das Unsagbare verstiess.
Es wurde Nacht im Paradies:
sei du der Hüter mit dem Horne,
und man erzählt nur, dass er blies.

The first word that you ever spoke was: light.
Thus time began. For long you said no more.
Man was your second, and a frightening, word
(the sound of it still shrouds us in its night),
and then again you brooded as before.

But I am one who would not hear your third.

I often pray at night: Be but the dumb,
confined to gestures, growing quietly,
he whom the spirit moves in dreams, that he
may write on speechless brows the heavy sum
of silence, and on peaks for us to see.

Be you the shelter from the angry scorn
that violated the ineffable.
In very paradise night fell:
be you the herdsman with the horn,
that once was blown, but so they only tell.

Es lärmt das Licht im Wipfel deines Baumes
und macht dir alle Dinge bunt und eitel,
sie finden dich erst, wenn der Tag verglomm.
Die Dämmerung, die Zärtlichkeit des Raumes,
legt tausend Hände über tausend Scheitel,
und unter ihnen wird das Fremde fromm.

Du willst die Welt nicht anders an dich halten
als so, mit dieser sanftesten Gebärde.
Aus ihren Himmeln greifst du dir die Erde
und fühlst sie unter deines Mantels Falten.

Du hast so eine leise Art zu sein.
Und jene, die dir laute Namen weihn,
sind schon vergessen deiner Nachbarschaft.
Von deinen Händen, die sich bergig heben,
steigt, unsern Sinnen das Gesetz zu geben,
mit dunkler Stirne deine stumme Kraft.

The light shouts in your tree-top, and the face
of all things becomes radiant and vain;
only at dusk do they find you again.
The twilight hour, the tenderness of space,
lays on a thousand heads a thousand hands,
and strangeness grows devout where they have lain.

With this gentlest of gestures you would hold
the world, thus only and not otherwise.
You lean from out its skies to capture earth,
and feel it underneath your mantle's folds.

You have so mild a way of being.
                                   They
who name you loudly when they come to pray
forget your nearness. From your hands that tower
above us, mountainously, lo, there soars,
to give the law whereby our senses live,
dark-browed, your wordless power.

Lösch mir die Augen aus: ich kann dich sehn,
wirf mir die Ohren zu: ich kann dich hören,
und ohne Füsse kann ich zu dir gehn,
und ohne Mund noch kann ich dich beschwören.
Brich mir die Arme ab, ich fasse dich
mit meinem Herzen wie mit einer Hand,
halt mir das Herz zu, und mein Hirn wird schlagen,
und wirfst du in mein Hirn den Brand,
so werd ich dich auf meinem Blute tragen.

Put out my eyes, and I can see you still;
slam my ears to, and I can hear you yet;
and without any feet can go to you;
and tongueless, I can conjure you at will.
Break off my arms, I shall take hold of you
and grasp you with my heart as with a hand;
arrest my heart, my brain will beat as true;
and if you set this brain of mine afire,
upon my blood I then will carry you.

Und doch, obwohl, ein jeder von sich strebt
wie aus dem Kerker, der ihn hasst und hält,—
es ist ein grosses Wunder in der Welt:
ich fühle: ALLES LEBEN WIRD GELEBT.
Wer lebt es denn? Sind das die Dinge, die
wie eine ungespielte Melodie
im Abend wie in einer Harfe stehn?
Sind das die Winde, die von Wassern wehn,
sind das die Zweige, die sich Zeichen geben,
sind das die Blumen, die die Düfte weben,
sind das die langen alternden Alleen?
Sind das die warmen Tiere, welche gehn,
sind das die Vögel, die sich fremd erheben?
Wer lebt es denn? Lebst du es, Gott,—das Leben?

Although, as from a prison walled with hate,
each from his own self labors to be free,
the world yet holds a wonder, and how great!
ALL LIFE IS LIVED: now this comes home to me.
But who, then, lives it? Things that patiently
stand there, like some unfingered melody
that sleeps within a harp as day is going?
Is it the winds, across the waters blowing,
is it the branches, beckoning each to each,
is it the flowers, weaving fragrances,
the ageing alleys that reach out endlessly?
Is it the warm beasts, moving to and fro,
is it the birds, strange as they sail from view?
This life—who lives it really? God, do you?

𝕯u bist die Zukunft, grosses Morgenrot
über den Ebenen der Ewigkeit.
Du bist der Hahnschrei nach der Nacht der Zeit,
der Tau, die Morgenmette und die Maid,
der fremde Mann, die Mutter und der Tod.

Du bist die sich verwandelnde Gestalt,
die immer einsam aus dem Schicksal ragt,
die unbejubelt bleibt und unbeklagt
und unbeschrieben wie ein wilder Wald.

Du bist der Dinge tiefer Inbegriff,
der seines Wesens letztes Wort verschweigt
und sich den andern immer anders zeigt:
dem Schiff als Küste und dem Land als Schiff.

You are the future, the great sunrise red
above the broad plains of eternity.
You are the cock-crow when time's night has fled,
You are the dew, the matins, and the maid,
the stranger and the mother, you are death.

You are the changeful shape that out of Fate
rears up in everlasting solitude,
the unlamented and the unacclaimed,
beyond describing as some savage wood.

You are the deep epitome of things
that keeps its being's secret with locked lip,
and shows itself to others otherwise:
to the ship, a haven—to the land, a ship.

Die Konige der Welt sind alt
und werden keine Erben haben.
Die Söhne sterben schon als Knaben,
und ihre bleichen Töchter gaben
die kranken Kronen der Gewalt.
Der Pöbel bricht sie klein zu Geld,
der zeitgemässe Herr der Welt
dehnt sie im Feuer zu Maschinen,
die seinem Wollen grollend dienen;
aber das Glück ist nicht mit ihnen.
Das Erz hat Heimweh. Und verlassen
will es die Münzen und die Räder,
die es ein kleines Leben lehren.
Und aus Fabriken und aus Kassen
wird es zurück in das Geäder
der aufgetanen Berge kehren,
die sich verschliessen hinter ihm.

The sovereigns of the world are old
and they will have no heirs at all.
Death took their sons when they were small,
and their pale daughters soon resigned
to force frail crowns they could not hold.
The mob breaks these to bits of gold
that the world's master, shrewd and bold,
melts in the fire to enginery
that sullenly serves his desires,
but fortune is not in his hire.
The ore is homesick. It is eager
to leave the coins and turning wheels
that offer it a life so meagre.
From coffers and from factories
it would flow back into the veins
of gaping mountains whence it came,
that close upon it once again.

Alles wird wieder gross sein und gewaltig,
die Lande einfach und die Wasser faltig,
die Bäume riesig und sehr klein die Mauern;
und in den Tälern, stark und vielgestaltig,
ein Volk von Hirten und von Ackerbauern.

Und keine Kirchen, welche Gott umklammern
wie einen Flüchtling und ihn dann bejammern
wie ein gefangenes und wundes Tier,—
die Häuser gastlich allen Einlassklopfern
und ein Gefühl von unbegrenztem Opfern
in allem Handeln und in dir und mir.

Kein Jenseitswarten und kein Schaun nach drüben,
nur Sehnsucht, auch den Tod nicht zu entweihn
und dienend sich am Irdischen zu üben,
um seinen Händen nicht mehr neu zu sein.

All will grow great and powerful again:
the seas be wrinkled and the land be plain,
the trees gigantic and the walls be low;
and in the valleys, strong and multiform,
a race of herdsmen and of farmers grow.

No churches to encircle God as though
he were a fugitive, and then bewail him
as if he were a captured wounded creature,—
all houses will prove friendly, there will be
a sense of boundless sacrifice prevailing
in dealings between men, in you, in me.

No waiting the beyond, no peering toward it,
but longing to degrade not even death;
we shall learn earthliness, and serve its ends,
to feel its hands about us like a friend's.

Jetzt reifen schon die roten Berberitzen,
alternde Astern atmen schwach im Beet.
Wer jetzt nicht reich ist, da der Sommer geht,
wird immer warten und sich nie besitzen.

Wer jetzt nicht seine Augen schliessen kann,
gewiss, dass eine Fülle von Gesichten
in ihm nur wartet, bis die Nacht begann,
um sich in seinem Dunkel aufzurichten:—
der ist vergangen wie ein alter Mann.

Dem kommt nichts mehr, dem stösst kein Tag mehr zu,
und alles lügt ihn an, was ihm geschieht;
auch du, mein Gott. Und wie ein Stein bist du,
welcher ihn täglich in die Tiefe zieht.

Already ripening barberries grow red,
the ageing asters scarce breathe in their bed.
Who is not rich, with summer nearly done,
will never find a self that is his own.

Who is unable now to close his eyes,
certain that many visages within
wait slumbering until night shall begin
and in the darkness of his soul will rise,
is like an aged man whose strength is gone.

Nothing will touch him in the days to come,
and each event will cheat him and betray,
even you, my God. And you are like a stone,
that draws him to a lower depth each day.

Du musst nicht bangen, Gott. Sie sagen: "mein"
zu allen Dingen, die geduldig sind.
Sie sind wie Wind der an die Zweige streift
und sagt: MEIN Baum.

Sie merken kaum,
wie alles glüht, was ihre Hand ergreift,—
so dass sie's auch an seinem letzten Saum
nicht halten könnten, ohne zu verbrennen.

Sie sagen mein, wie manchmal einer gern
den Fürsten Freund nennt im Gespräch mit Bauern,
wenn dieser Fürst sehr gross ist und—sehr fern.
Sie sagen mein von ihren fremden Mauern
und kennen gar nicht ihres Hauses Herrn.
Sie sagen mein und nennen das Besitz,
wenn jedes Ding sich schliesst, dem sie sich nahn
so wie ein abgeschmackter Scharlatan
vielleicht die Sonne sein nennt und den Blitz.
So sagen sie: mein Leben, meine Frau,
mein Hund, mein Kind, und wissen doch genau,
das alles: Leben, Frau und Hund und Kind
fremde Gebilde sind, daran sie blind
mit ihren ausgestreckten Händen stossen.
Gewissheit freilich ist das nur den Grossen,
die sich nach Augen sehnen. Denn die andern

𝔇o not be troubled, God, though they say "mine"
of all things that permit it patiently.
They are like wind that lightly strokes the boughs
and says: MY tree.

They hardly see
how all things glow that their hands seize upon,
so that they cannot touch
even the utmost fringe and not be singed.

They will say "mine" as one will sometimes call
the prince his friend in speech with villagers,
this prince being very great—and far away.
They call strange walls "mine," knowing not at all
who is the master of the house indeed.
They still say "mine," and claim possession, though
each thing, as they approach, withdraws and closes;
a silly charlatan perhaps thus poses
as owner of the lightning and the sun.
And so they say: my life, my wife, my child,
my dog, well knowing all that they have styled
their own: life, wife, child, dog, remain
shapes foreign and unknown,
that blindly groping they must stumble on.
This truth, be sure, only the great discern,
who long for eyes. The others WILL not learn

WOLLEN's nicht hören, dass ihr armes Wandern
mit keinem Dinge rings zusammenhängt,
dass sie, von ihrer Habe fortgedrängt,
nicht anerkannt von ihrem Eigentume,
das Weib so wenig HABEN wie die Blume,
die eines fremden Lebens ist für alle.

Falle nicht, Gott, aus deinem Gleichgewicht.
Auch der dich liebt und der dein Angesicht
erkennt im Dunkel, wenn er wie ein Licht
in deinem Atem schwankt,—besitzt dich nicht.
Und wenn dich einer in der Nacht erfasst,
so dass du kommen musst in sein Gebet:
    Du bist der Gast,
      der wieder weitergeht.

Wer kann dich halten, Gott? Denn du bist dein,
von keines Eigentümers Hand gestört,
so wie der noch nicht ausgereifte Wein,
der immer süsser wird, sich selbst gehört.

that in the beggary of their wandering
they cannot claim a bond with any thing,
but, driven from possessions they have prized,
not by their own belongings recognized,
they can OWN wives no more than they own flowers,
whose life is alien and apart from ours.

God, do not lose your equilibrium.
Even he who loves you and discerns your face
in darkness, when he trembles like a light
you breathe upon,—he cannot own you quite.
And if at night one holds you closely pressed,
locked in his prayer so you cannot stray,

     you are the guest
     who comes, but not to stay.

God, who can hold you? To yourself alone
belonging, by no owner's hand disturbed,
you are like unripened wine that unperturbed
grows ever sweeter and is all its own.

Some New Directions Paperbooks

Complete descriptive catalog available free on request from
New Directions, 80 Eighth Avenue, New York 10011   † Bilingual